WELCOME

So you're looking to buy a new home? Congratulations! You're about to embark on a worthwhile yet stressful journey. Whether you're purchasing a new home because inventory is low, you're sick of getting outbid, or you've always dreamt of a new build, you'll need help navigating the tumultuous process, and that's where I come in.

It took me roughly 12,960 hours working in new construction to realize two things: I had become an expert in the industry and I absolutely hated it. My ultimate life goal is to help people. I thought working in new home sales would accomplish that. What's more fulfilling than helping people build their dreams? I loved assisting excited buyers at the start, but the magic didn't last long. That initial high turned into anxiety and shame, as their expectations fell short. I tried my best to guide people through the process, but at the end of the day, I represented the builder.

I was always delighted when one of our buyers had an agent with experience in new construction. Unfortunately, this was not the norm. Most of the time I had to coach the agent on the entire process. Even as I transitioned to resale as a Realtor® in Los Angeles, I can confirm that very few of my colleagues have done a transaction with a production builder.

If you need more evidence, I recently contacted 40 homeowners from three different production builders, purchasing from around the country. I asked them to highlight their pain points about the process and how straightforward it was. Of those 40 people, only one person said their experience matched the outlined expectations.

Okay, so I can't guarantee you won't lose your mind, but I can help you prepare. To be clear, the intention of this guide is not to trash production builders or discredit agents. It's a home-buying guide designed to help you before you step foot into a model home up until the contract. It is based on my accounts of working in new home sales for a production builder in Colorado and California, as well as insights from builders, agents, loan officers, and buyers across the country.

While this may not be an exact step-by-step guide for your specific builder, it's a handy tool filled with insider knowledge to give you a strong foundation. I'm happy to be a medium that doesn't have anything to gain or lose should you choose to buy a new home or resale. In fact, I may be the only medium you will have. I hope to shed light on the process with brutal honesty to set proper expectations. My goal of this guide is to equip you with the knowledge to create a better home buying experience. Thank you for letting me do what I do best - help you.

CHRISTINA ZAMORA

A LIGHT IN DARK PLACES

PLAYS FOR HOPE

THANK YOU!

A portion of the proceeds from this book will be donated to A Light In Dark Places. ALIDP is a non-profit using the arts for suicide prevention while creating a community, resources, and hope for those affected by suicide.

Connect

www.alightindarkplaces.org

⊙ @alightindarkplaces

CONTENT

CHRISTINA ZAMORA | @thechristinazamora

CONTENT

CHRISTINA ZAMORA | @thechristinazamora

PROPER EXPECTATIONS

Buying a home, new or resale, is one of the most important decisions you will ever make. It's right up there with marriage and having a baby. Though often idealized, purchasing a new construction home from a production builder is not for everyone.

It's easy to get sucked in by the perfectly curated Instagram photos that display "SOLD" flashing across your screen. However, what you don't see are the challenges behind the scenes to get to that point. So before you make any decisions, it's best to evaluate the pros and cons of new construction versus resale. Here is a quick comparison.

NEW   RESALE

TIMING

✓ 4+ Months (unless an existing build is available).

✗ Delays are expected.

✗ Closing date is not confirmed until ~30 days prior to closing.

✓ 30-45 Day Close.

FINANCING

✓ Interest rate isn't locked in until 45-60 days until closing.

✓ Earnest money is put down at sign of contract but is credited toward your down payment at closing. This can give time to save additional funds & lenders can prequalify you for more with that in mind.

✗ Lock interest rates immediately.

✗ Need proof of funds.

PRICING

✓ No negotiation - home prices depends on the market.

✗ Pricing is vague. The initial price is before upgrades and you may not know the final until after contract.

✓ Can submit offers.

✓ Pricing is very clear.

COMMUNITY

✓ Everyone is a newcomer.

✓ New amenities.

✗ Inconvenience of construction (potential nail in tires, constant noise).

✗ Can't neighborhood search future neighbors.

✓ No construction.

✓ Area has been developed: (Internet and power lines installed, etc.)

✓ Can see how neighbors live.

✗ Established neighbors.

NEW	RESALE

UPGRADES

NEW	RESALE
✓ Ability to upgrade and include it in your mortgage.	✓ Home has settled.
✓ Meet with a professional designer.	✓ Landscaping has matured- allowing more privacy.
✓ Warranties on appliances.	✓ Landscaping is established.
✗ Limited to builder's design options.	✗ Any home improvements/changes are out of pocket.
✗ Most don't offer custom options. They stick to what is offered and often let you "personalize."	
✗ Additional deposit for upgrades may be required.	
✗ 100% expectation of level of what is considered standard is not initially clear.	
✗ Potentially responsible for backyard landscaping after closing.	

SURPRISES

NEW	RESALE
✓ Expect them!	✓ Expect them!

The term 'new build' often lures home buyers into a false sense of security, where they start to equate the word "new" with "perfect." That notion couldn't be further from the truth, yet it's a believable pitch. For instance, the sales rep might say, "Buy new because, with a resale house, you could move in and have your water heater break the next day." The truth is you could move into a new home and have your water heater break. The primary difference between the two is that a new build will likely have a warranty.

The bottom line is whether you're purchasing a new home or resale, issues will arise, and it's best to anticipate that to avoid disappointment.

IS NEW CONSTRUCTION FOR ME?

☐ Is my timeline flexible?

☐ I am not interested in doing a custom build.

☐ Do I want to personalize my home?

☐ Do I understand a new home does not mean a perfect home?

☐ Am I okay with delays?

☐ Am I okay with knowing my community may be a construction site after I move in?

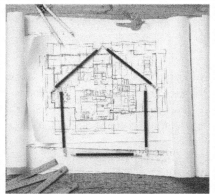

If you said yes to all of the above, let's get started on the process of getting you into a new construction home!

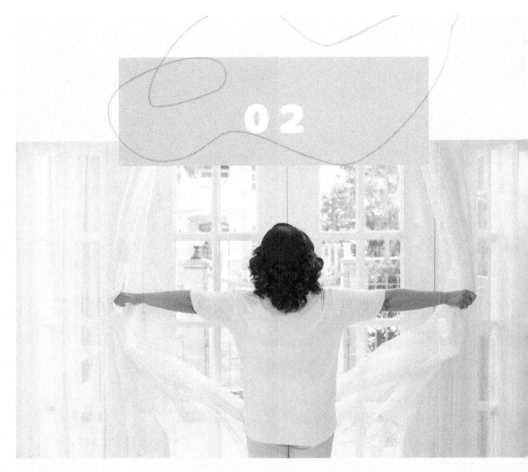

UNICORN HOME

Ah, the magical unicorn home. Agents internally use this term when their buyer is looking for a home that checks off all the boxes without any compromise. To be clear, you should never settle on a home, but the reality of waiting around for the perfect one is simply unrealistic.

Compromise is necessary even if you purchase a new construction home. The only way to fulfill every aspect of your wishlist is through a custom-build, but that comes with a hefty price. Production builders aren't able to offer the same benefits as custom-build homes, but they do offer add-ons and other specifics. You'll have a chance to discuss all of this with the builder at their design center or with the sales rep.

The benefit of working with production builders is that their floor plans are designed to be functional and therefore, appeal to the masses. Whereas a custom home may only be attractive to a select few. If you want everything custom but a custom home is currently out of your budget, don't let that deter you from making moves. Instead, use a production-build home as a stepping stone to your custom dream home. This will help you build equity and increase your long-term buying power.

Now before we get into the steps of purchasing new construction, let's take a moment to reflect on what your goal is and uncover your "why" for initiating the home buying process. This is a major purchase and taking time to write down your needs, wants and reasons will help guide you toward the right decision.

Next, make a list of your non-negotiable items, followed by your nice-to-haves. Also, feel free to ask for help or feedback from a sales representative. They can provide insight and offer alternative solutions. For example, let's say you are looking for a home with enough space for a pool. Do you need the largest lot in the community to build it? Probably not.

HOME SWEET HOME

Let's get organized! Sometimes it's difficult to determine what is an absolute "need" in your ideal home and what is more of a "want." Below, write down a list of items that you would like for your next home and run through the exercise of asking yourself, "Why do I need this?" Or "Is it more of a want?"

IN MY FUTURE HOME	NEED?	WANT?	WHY?

PRE-GAME

Congratulations! Now that you've narrowed down what you're looking for, you're one step closer to moving into your new home! The excitement can send you running out the door, but there are a few items to line up before setting foot in a sales office.

First, find a Realtor® you can trust and rely on. You technically don't need a Realtor® for new construction, but I promised to be completely honest with you, so take my advice and get a Realtor®! Once you've found representation, get in touch with a lender to get pre-qualified.

FIND A REALTOR®

For clarity, agents you meet at the model home sales office who work for the builder are called sales reps. The agent who represents you in the purchasing process is your Realtor®. As previously discussed, few Realtors® work on new construction homes. Let's discuss why.

The time it takes from start to close on a new build could be several months, with minimal commission. Not to mention, challenges and potential delays often arise. On top of that, early 2021 reports show that many builders have reduced commissions to 2% versus the 2.5-3% commission rate on a resale home.

Another challenge is finding new construction homes. Realtors® often rely on the MLS (multiple listing service) for finding available homes, but new construction isn't always listed. It just depends on the builder and traffic. In the past working for a builder, I've listed homes on the MLS if they needed extra exposure. Fast forward to mid-2020, where I had no use for the MLS because houses sold out immediately. I had waiting lists of more than 40 people in a community with 35 homes left. So it can be tricky for Realtors® to find new construction if they're not local to the area.

With all that said, if you find a community on your own and even pick out a floor plan, the sales rep might advise you to forgo a Realtor®. Should you still get one anyway? YES

Most sales reps you meet in model homes have a real estate license (depending on the state). They are experts on their product and should be used as a resource to help understand what you're purchasing. However, don't forget they represent the builder, not you. In fact, many builder purchase agreements state exactly that.

Sales reps are also juggling multiple customers at a time, making it difficult for them to focus solely on you. At times I had more than 40 buyers under contract with increasing pressure to land my next sale.

Hiring a Realtor® is no cost to you. When purchasing a home the seller pays the agent. As a side note, you will not receive the commission if you don't have an agent (it's always asked).

So does hiring a Realtor® help with the negotiation? Not exactly. There is little to no negotiation involved when working with a builder. There can be exceptions when the market is slower. With that in mind, it doesn't hurt to ask. The main reason you want a Realtor® is to have someone on your side.

If you're starting from dirt, there are at least 150 days for something to inevitably pop up. I have assisted in more than 300 closings and I can promise you that not one transaction was the same. THINGS POP UP. When they do, you'll want someone to represent you.

Builders are quick to tell the buyer no. To make matters worse, contractually speaking, the purchase agreement is written to protect the builder. In a slower market, builders need you. They will be more attentive and in your corner. In hot markets, the builders are understaffed to maintain their budget. I've heard builders say numerous times, "if the buyer is unhappy they can walk away." This usually means losing your earnest money (via a security deposit), which could be a big portion of your down payment. Who wants to walk away from that?

This is where I felt gross in my position. There were times I threw a fit in order to get something done after the builder told me no. Sometimes I was successful in my endeavor, but not always. Additionally, not all sales reps are willing to do that, as it puts their job in jeopardy. A sales rep's relationship with their manager is critical to their next placement and it could be the difference of thousands of dollars or even cost their job.

I can't stress enough that new construction sales reps work for the builder. They are managed by a manager who is managed by someone above them and so on. Their ultimate goal is to please the shareholders. You, as the buyer, will need someone to represent you and your interests. Builders consider a Realtor® as nothing more than a referral, but it's more than that. Realtors® can make noise and will push the builder to complete talks on behalf of you because they want to close. For example, I saw the builder trying to do a final walk on homes without countertops in. The agent escalated this quickly. They can also be a source of comfort during the tough process. You should be selective. Choose a team that is fully behind you and whom you trust.

Here's a great example of a first-time buyer who would have benefited from a Realtor®. The buyer went under contract right before the community gained in popularity. Two months before closing they got cold feet. I tried to be transparent and let the buyer know that walking away was a big mistake, but they needed someone else. Ultimately, the builder kept their deposit of $11,000 and turned around and sold their lot the next day for almost $40,000 more. If the original buyer had someone they trusted on their side, they wouldn't have walked away.

CHRISTINA ZAMORA | @thechristinazamora

CHOOSE A REALTOR
WITH EXPERIENCE

There are benefits to having someone on your team who is familiar with the process of new construction. It's even better if they previously sold a new build. With all the information that is thrown at you, it helps to have someone who understands standards vs upgrades, the building process, financing, and how to complete a walkthrough.

Make sure you talk to your agent and set expectations on their involvement. Starting the new build process is time-consuming. You can't expect your agent to go with you every time you want to visit the builder's site, but make sure they are present for any big decisions.

For instance, your Realtor® should accompany you during your first visit to the builder or whenever you fill out a registration card. Since the Realtor® is technically a referral, the builder will want them to be the procuring cause. If your Realtor® can't be present, let the sales rep know you have one. It's a good idea to keep your Realtor® information handy on your phone.

If you're having trouble finding a Realtor®, go check out the neighborhood you're considering on a weekend. Your future neighbors will likely be out and about so you can ask around for a referral. You got this!

CONTINGENCY

If you have a house that needs to be sold in order to buy a new home this is called a contingency. In this case, you should be prepared with a CMA of your current home.

A common misconception with new builds is that you don't have to sell your current house right away, since your new home won't be ready for months. This is wrong. Builders want little to no grey area in a deal. After all, they are fronting around 98% of the cost to build your home. They're not going to move forward with the hope that you'll be able to sell your house seven months from now.

So if you have home improvements you've been putting off, start on those now. If you do not qualify for both homes, you will have to list and close your current home in a set amount of time per the builder contract. I saw timeframes of listing within seven days of signing with the builder and being under contract within 60 days. If your house doesn't sell within the contingency period, you're entitled to a refund (always double-check the contract for terms).

Now if you have a build time on your new home for six months, this means your current home will close before you can move into your new one. So where do you live in the meantime? Short-term leases are often expensive and hard to find. Many people make a sacrifice and move in with family or friends. Though inconvenient, this can help you save more money for the down payment.

Planning a double move is almost unavoidable if you have to sell your home. You can talk to your agent about listing with a leaseback, but it depends on the market climate if someone will accept it. Another route you could take is through the builder, but it's risky. The builder may have an option to make your money hard. This costs much more than a regular deposit and is non-refundable. I saw 5%. Basically, you are betting that your current house will sell by the time you close on your new build. No one has a crystal ball so this option is not generally recommended.

CHRISTINA ZAMORA | @thechristinazamora

DO'S & DON'TS OF WORKING WITH A REALTOR:

- ✔ Have one!

- ✔ Have your agent send you a picture of their card.

- ✔ When visiting builders' sales offices, tell them you are working with an agent.

- ✔ Give the builder's sales representative your agent's information.

- ✖ Set expectations that your agent isn't always available to go to every builder visit.

- ✔ Keep your agents looped in on walk-throughs and relay any important information.

Let's go get pre-qualified!

GET PRE-QUALIFIED

Many people think they don't need to get prequalified before looking for a new home because closing could take several months. The reality is once you begin looking, the builder's timeline will be months out as well and may even line up with your move. However, a must-have to get started is a pre-qualification.

When buyers learn about getting prequalified, sometimes their first instinct is to move full speed ahead, without taking time to consider their finances. Many builders offer incentives for using their in-house lender. This is a great option that most buyers take advantage of. However, builders may have different in-house lenders and it's not a good idea to apply to all of them, as each time your credit will get hit. Now, if your credit is pulled within a certain period, it all gets grouped together as opposed to several different hits. The best course of action is to talk to an outside lender first to understand your buying power.

Once equipped with this knowledge, you will learn if a house is truly out of your price range. This may seem obvious, but it is not uncommon for sales reps (who are under pressure to meet a goal) to take you to contract without being prequalified. This is a setup for failure and disappointment.

When you sign the contract to move forward, you're not required to pay the full down payment, but a portion called earnest money. This is held in escrow and credited toward your down payment at closing. Many people don't realize this and hold off on looking until they have their full down payment. By that point, people are annoyed by the build times and settle for something already on the market. This is something you want to discuss with your lender.

CHRISTINA ZAMORA|CHRISTINA@.REMAXENVISION.COM

For example, let's say you want to be closed on a home in 5 months from now. If you don't have your full down payment yet but can show proof of the rate you are saving at they may be able to prequalify you.

Pre-Qualification Amount

When you get prequalified, it should come with a cushion. A new build allows you to customize your home, which adds to the total price. Discuss this with your lender and ask what your payments would be for a max purchase price at a cushioned interest. Due to the way builders price homes, you shouldn't look for homes that start with your max. It is common homes finish at a minimum of $40,000 more than the base price.

Interest Rate and Payments

Your interest rate is an important variable and should be discussed with your lender. Lenders can provide a prequalification with only a dollar amount, but that is unreliable and confusing. For example, if you are prequalified at a high rate and rates are trending down, that could lower your payments. On the other hand, if you are given a low rate and rates increase by the time you close, you may not have a home!

You can easily Google what interest rates are currently and while this is good practice, there are other variables at play. Your qualifying interest rate is determined by your credit score, loan program, down payment, debt to income ratio, and more.

New build communities often have HOA's and special assessments. It is common now certain areas even require solar. These are all factors that will effect your payments and what you qualify for.

Make sure you have all of this information to give to your lender so you can have a clear idea of what your payments will look like. The only variable should be your interest rate, which unfortunately you don't lock in until nearly closing.

IN HOUSE LENDER

Once you choose your community, floor plan, and have secured a lot, you may want to apply to the in-house lender. This lending affiliate is not directly employed by the builder, but the builder typically does receive referral compensation.

Compare the in-house lender's offer with your own. Keep in mind that a builder can't force you to use their lender, so do not feel obligated. However, there could be benefits of working with an in-house lender, such as a closing cost incentive. These are funds you have to fork over at closing, and many outside lenders can't compete with that deal.

New homes have a higher closing cost than resale, with the price varying by the lender. They can be around 3% of the total price or more. To put that into perspective, on a $500,000 house that is $15,000! So regardless of how you know your lender, they will understand if you go with the in-house lender to save money. It's tough to end a friendly business relationship, but you have to do what makes sense financially.

There is a catch. Free is not always free. The in-house lender's rate could be higher, so it depends if you want to save money upfront or in the long run. Also, many in-house lenders are conservative because they sell the loans. They are looking for basic, FHA, conventional, or VA buyers with good credit and low debt to income ratios. If that's not you, then you better have a backup lender.

Fair warning that many builder's preferred lenders will have terrible reviews. You'll start to question why anyone would use them. Set your expectations low in regards to their customer service. The loan officers (LO) are dealing with triple the number of loans than the average LO and aren't incentivized to deliver stellar customer service.

From my experience, closing delays can occur from in-house lenders, but typically the builder will not charge a late per diem if it's their fault. The opposite happens when you use an outside lender.

LATE FEES

If you decide to go with an outside lender, the home must be closed by the builder's closing date. Builders will often charge a per diem past the closing day. I have witnessed over $10,000 in charges ($255/day) because a lender couldn't close.

Unfortunately, It's your responsibility to stay on top of your lender to ensure a timely close. I can't stress enough how important it is to manage this loan process to avoid unnecessary costs. Make sure to thoroughly discuss this before you decide on a lender. Ask lots of questions, including if they've done new construction before.

When I spoke with the LO of my buyer who got charged over $10,000, he mentioned how he hates working with builders and has done few deals with them previously. This would have been pertinent information for my buyers to know ahead of time.

Don't let this process intimidate you. You got this! Many people have a hard time with financing. Watching someone lose their home on closing day, after months of construction and $15,000 later, all because of miscommunication is heartbreaking. It can be prevented!

The more you know the better. Digging into your finances can feel intimidating and uncomfortable, but once you know where you stand, you're able to finally start your search.

DO'S & DON'TS OF GETTING PRE-QUALIFIED:

- ✖ Don't start your search until you've talked to your lender.
- ✔ Do get qualified for the max amount.
- ✔ Understand what your monthly payment would be.
- ✔ Have your lender budget property taxes, HOA fees, and home insurance into your payments.
- ✔ Cross qualify once you have decided on the builder

Once this is complete, it's time to find your NEW home!

SEARCH IS ON

Houses are typically found on the MLS by Realtors®. However, new communities are often not included in the MLS. Production builders market new communities themselves and use street signage to draw attention.

Buyers often become deterred by seeing a lonely trailer on a pile of dirt. However, there are advantages of getting into a community in the early phases, such as increasing your equity. Builders will increase the price of homes based on the demand of the market and the inventory available. Don't wait to visit the office until there are homes up!

If you're looking at a builder that offers more in-depth personalization, they'll want you to choose everything. Personalization adds to their profit and the builder is

confident building the home because they already have an invested buyer. These build times will be longer, as they won't start construction until it is under contract.

Other builders are more focused on pushing units and will build houses with the option of selective final personalizations (countertops and flooring) and a quicker close.

Some builders take an "everything is included" approach. This may come off nice up front knowing the exact price but could cost you in the end. If you go with an all-inclusive builder but want to start making changes once you close escrow, it's going to cost you. You'll have to pay for the changes out of pocket and deal with a construction zone. It could even jeopardize some of your warranties. If you go with a personalized builder and want to make changes, you will only be paying for the difference between the upgrade and the standard base option.

If you are looking at a builder that is not all-inclusive, be aware that the signage pricing is not your final price. The starting price point is the base price of the lowest-priced floor plan. You never get a house at the base price. Base + lot premium + structural options = final price. We'll discuss this more later, but the takeaway here is that paying attention to pricing can save you time and frustration.

If you are open to living in several different cities, then driving around to look for signs is a waste of time. There aren't many helpful websites, but one that stands out is Buzzbuzzhome.com. It has a helpful map of new home communities and even connects you with a vetted real estate agent.

If you come across a builder or community you're interested in, check out their website! There's often a live chat feature, which you should take advantage of. There is a human behind this chat who likely works at the builder's main office. They know all about the current communities, inventory, and even upcoming projects. They get paid for setting appointments and get a bonus when you sign. They'll make an effort to follow up and ensure the sales agent took care of you.

Instead of calling communities within a builder individually, use the live chat to connect to the builder and have them set up a whole day with appointments at your convenience.
Appointments aren't required to view model homes, but sometimes they are preferred. If you happen to be in the area and want to stop in, don't be intimidated! Worst case scenario is they tell you to make an appointment.

PRODUCTION BUILDER REVIEWS

Similar to the lender reviews, production builders aren't much better. They can be entertaining to read, but not if you're trying to buy. So why would someone choose a builder with one star? There's a lot that can happen in a build, so it's important to remember this.

For starters, it's more likely for upset customers to post reviews than happy ones. Also, builders are generally over-producing and working with a small team. If you decide to dive down the review rabbit hole, pay attention to where these people live. I noticed a huge difference between working in Colorado and California with the same company! The process, trades, economics, and environment were vastly different and can impact the build significantly. I've seen reviews from people that live in various states with problems I've never encountered in California. Even on a microlevel, it can vary by cities!

The builder's name is attached to the homes, and a builder-employed superintendent oversees it. However, the houses are only as good as the trades (electricians, framers, drywall contractors, and painters) they hire. If you want my best advice, visit the community's park and talk to someone. If no one has moved in yet, ask where the closest community with similar floorplans is. Neighboring communities often use similar trades and could be a good way to gauge the quality of work. So get out there and talk to your future neighbors!

DO'S & DON'TS OF FINDING A COMMUNITY:

- ✖ Don't ignore properties that haven't started building.

- ✔ Do your research on local builders.

- ✔ Decide if a longer build with more personalization is for you.

- ✔ Use resources on builders' websites to set up appointments.

- ✔ Talk to those who live in the neighborhood to get a better sense of the community!

Let's get started!

VISTING COMMUNITIES

This part of the process can be overwhelming, but it can also be fun! Take careful note of the presented model homes. This is where the builder shows all of the bells and whistles you can add, at a premium price tag of course. Expect that everything you see in a model home is the upgraded version. If on the off chance it's included, that's just a bonus for you.

When you arrive at the sales office you will likely be greeted by a sales rep. Talk to them! This person has all of the answers and both of you want to make a good impression. Sales reps are trained to ask you questions to determine if their community is where you're looking to buy. Let them ask questions, but don't feel pressured into anything. Sales reps are experts on their product, and they may have already crossed off two floor plans that won't work for you.

If they suggest starting with a certain model, take their advice. By the time you tour your third model, they will all start to blend together. Also, it's easy to get dazzled by the designer upgrades and swanky furniture, but stay focused on the layout. Depending on the day and traffic, the sales rep may want to walk you through the models. If it's your first time there and you prefer to look on your own, let them know.

I was trained to walk people through on their first visit. I hated this and felt it was pushy and overwhelming. I found a good flow was to let people walk once to understand the floorplan then later I would walk with them to discuss upgrades. The importance of walking with the sales agent at some point before going to contract should not be overlooked. Do not forget to do this!

They'll also want you to fill out a registration card to follow up with you. Builders expect you to include your agent's information. If your agent is not present, inform the sales team that you are working with an agent. Sometimes they'll cooperate with you by putting your agent's info on the card. However, if the sales rep insists that your agent be present, you can kindly decline to provide your information.

Before heading out to the models, ask for floor plans, pricing, and a pen. Agents often like to hand out pricing at the end so you don't rule anything out. Their logic here is if you fall in love with a floor plan, you'll make it happen. I found it upsetting to watch people bend over backward to become house poor, so don't make that mistake. Also, keep in mind that unless your builder is all-inclusive, there are always additional charges to the base price.

WALKING THE MODELS

Before you step into the first model, take a look at the exterior. This is called the elevation. Each floor plan usually has a few different elevations. Although the community may have three models, the houses don't look exactly the same because of the elevations.

Some elevations may be included and others will be an additional charge as a structural option. Elevations are predetermined in some communities and others give buyers a choice, but it's usually first come first serve. Elevations should be clearly listed on the provided floor plan.

The garage may not be on the same side as the model home. If the side of the garage changes the layout reverses. It's called a reverse layout. This often depends on the lot and is predetermined.

Another feature to take note of is the model home's landscaping. Typically front yard landscaping is included. However, model homes are not an example of the standard look. If you want a better idea of what the standard landscaping looks like, check out some of the finished homes in the neighborhood.

You will also notice that some homes include solar. Some states are making this a requirement. If the builder doesn't include solar in the price, you have the option to purchase or lease it. If purchased, it would be wrapped into your mortgage. If you lease it, this would be an additional monthly cost (you'll want to run this by your lender).

If the sales rep didn't tell you what model to start with, I recommend starting with the smallest one that meets your minimum bedroom requirement. Models constantly play tricks on your eyes. If you work from big to small, they might seem smaller than they actually are. It's best to start small and work your way up.

When you walk through the model, take notes of what you like and don't like in each floor plan. Don't wait until the end to try and remember. Pay attention to windows, doors, kitchen configurations, and more. The main structural options should be provided on the floor plans, which is a great way to determine what's standard.

The first round of your walkthrough should be dedicated to finding the layout that fits you best. Don't escape through the front gate once you're done (unless you hate the place). Check back in with the sales rep and ask them some questions to gauge the market and community. If the market is hot, you can inquire about waiting lists.

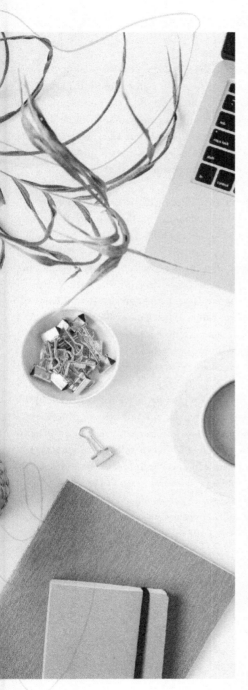

WAITING LISTS

The housing market varies and often dictates what the process looks like for sales reps.

If inventory is high in the resale market that means less business for new construction. This gives sales reps more free time to follow up with you and network with other agents to meet their goals.

When inventory is low in the resale market, the competition gets fierce and buyers are often outbid. So they flood into new construction to find a home instead. Sales reps will have less time to follow up with you, as now they have a line of people looking for a house.

I have worked on the extreme ends of both markets and everything in between. There were times I was calling old leads up to a year old. Most recently, in mid-2020, I had waiting lists upwards of 40 people in a community. I didn't have to follow up with anyone because people were following up with me.

The amount of business was unprecedented and it was clear there was no system in place to handle it. Every community and builder was handling its waiting list differently. If this is the market you're dealing with, then take note of how your builder is handling the process.

Sales reps will often want a prequalification letter to put you on the waiting list. Keep it on

your phone so you can easily email it. They may also ask for a deposit, but most states do not allow this. If you like the community, don't leave without putting yourself on the list! I watched people miss out and incur thousands in price increases because they didn't get on the list during their initial visit.

Don't give up hope if you are far down on the list. It could be the first person on the list or the 15th that gets the home. People move on.

Also, some builders will hold lotteries. If you're prequalified you can enter the lottery. The winner is chosen and contacted on the day of the lot release. This makes life easy for the sales rep, although it's not always fair. Someone who started looking yesterday could be chosen over someone looking for months.

There's a lot at stake price-wise as well. In this market, the price can increase significantly from the time you put your name on the list to the release. Prices typically go up with every release, which is about four to six houses. I would see $3,000 to $5,000 in increases for every two to three sales, not by releases. This is another reason you can't look at homes that start at your max prequalification price.

When it comes to contacting people on the waiting list in a hot market, don't expect more than one call and email. If buyers didn't get back to me right away, I was on to the next because I had people standing in my office asking to move forward.

When I had cancellations, I would follow up with people who were top of mind. This includes people who followed up regularly and who were nice to me. A few people sent emails that included a description of them or something memorable. For example, the crazy Disney fans, or the couple decked out in Bronco gear. It was helpful to remember who they were, considering I saw more than 30 families a day.

Buyers with Realtors® who actively followed up were helpful as well. An extra player on your team goes a long way. If a sales rep keeps calling you because you're on their list and you're no longer interested. Let them know you've moved on, so you don't waste anyone's time.

BUILD TIME

The chance of you finding the perfect home with a 30 to 45-day close is not good. If you want to personalize your home, it'll take even longer. You will receive a time range for your build, but it could change for any reason, including trades, weather conditions, corporate sales goals, supply shortage, and more. The supply shortage has been a common trend in 2020 and 2021 thus far.

So you won't have a solid idea of when your home will close until about a month out. Even with a set date, the builder could always move it. Also, don't expect the builder to pay for a moving truck or fees related to delays. You need to understand this so you can plan your move accordingly.

LOTS & UPGRADES
BASE + LOT PREMIUM+STRUCTURAL OPTIONS=FINAL PRICE

So you've narrowed down the community and floor plan! Here's where the expensive part comes in. The lot and upgrades are often what determines if people can afford a neighborhood or not. According to buyers, this is the most frustrating part of the process.

Upgraded items can add up quickly. So before you make any decisions, check back in with your "needs versus wants" list. It's easy to get carried away, but this list will help keep you grounded and stay within your budget.

LOTS

If you like a specific floor plan, see which upcoming lots can accommodate it. Ask if the lot premiums are available. If they don't have that information, ask for an estimate. Lot premiums are how much the land costs.

If the lot is not released yet, the sales rep won't know the exact price because it's determined by corporate right before the release. The price can fluctuate based on sales and location. If it is a more desirable location (corner lot, big backyard, or view), then expect a larger premium.

If a big backyard is important to you, ask for a map with dimensions. On average, new builds have smaller backyards than older homes, but they are still functional. A lot of people think they want a big backyard, but once they realize how much maintenance it requires, they change their minds.

You can also still do a lot with a smaller backyard. Even if you want a pool, you don't need the largest lot in the community to build one. Plus, new communities offer a ton of amenities! There's often a clubhouse, parks, gardens, and sports equipment. Enjoy these!

Marketing lot maps are just squares that aren't true to size. Don't focus only on the lot size because it can be misleading. A lot that is 9,000 square feet might have less usable space than a 5,000 sq lot.

If your goal is to have a big backyard, then you want to know the distance from the house line to the fence line for depth. Also, is the lot flat, or does it have a slope? Corner lots tend to have the greater square footage, but the bulk of it is not usable space.

People will often point to a large lot and say, "call me when this is released." They don't realize this is a disservice to them because by the time that lot is released, it won't be the same price. When this happens buyers go into sticker shock and end up walking away.

I watched this happen constantly to lots where the price shot up by $30,000 within a few months. The builder knows that people wait for certain lots, but it's a lose-lose situation for the buyer. This goes back to the unicorn home theory. What are you willing to compromise?

I recommend keeping an open mind on lots. It's hard to imagine how the house will look on a dirt lot. Your eyes play tricks. If they've already started digging, it's even harder to picture because they often over dig to accommodate for the foundation pour. Usually, lots are set up so that every other house will have a larger driveway. I've watched people pay hefty premiums on lots that seem great, but end up having less usable space than a standard lot.

Ask for a lot exhibit that shows the following: length of your driveway, garage placement (this affects your layout inside), distance from house to fence line, distance from patio to fence line, left and right

neighbors, drainage flow, and more. These numbers don't mean anything unless you compare them to something. Ask for the lot exhibit on the model home. Then walk the model lots and compare distances.

UPGRADES

If your builder offers personalization, you'll want to be clear about what's included, so you don't get your hopes up.

It's hard to believe you can't change something when you are still looking at an unfinished house. Once options are finalized there really is no going back because it takes a while for changes to be approved internally. Once they are, it gets uploaded to a separate system for construction. Construction has to order everything. So if something gets changed and construction doesn't have the right information, the wrong item will get installed.

That's why there is a huge difference between a production builder and a custom builder. Once you sign with a production builder, the countdown to close is on. They have a business plan and stick to it. The two upgrade options are classified as structural upgrades and home gallery upgrades. Builders will often require deposits on at least one.

Structural upgrades include your bedroom and bathroom configurations, windows, fireplaces, doors, kitchen layouts, morning rooms, basements, and more. Sit down with the sales rep and go over the structural options room by room. These upgrades have to be chosen at contract because they can affect the permit, foundation, and lumber package.

I recently spoke with a buyer about her experience with structural options. She told me she didn't understand what a specific structural option was and assumed she didn't need it. She later realized and wanted to upgrade, but it was too late. So ask questions. Many of these structural upgrades affect options at the home gallery and once you're there you can't make changes.

The home gallery or design center (builders have different names for it) is where everything is picked out after contract. You may have previewed some home galley samples during your first visit to the sales office. They typically have standard countertops, flooring, and cabinets available for preview.

Remember, models always display the most expensive upgrades. People expect to get the model home with maybe standard cabinets and countertops, but that's far from reality because there are many more options.

The sales reps may not even have a price range for what the model homes cost. The only way to discover the real price is at the design center, which you only get to visit after you sign your contract. People often feel swindled by this process. It is important to go in with a budget and know you may not get everything.

The design center has a ton of options, with multiple variations for each option. Vendors are constantly changing their prices, which affects the builder's price as well. Most design center appointments are broken up into two, four to six-hour appointments. This personalization process is so extensive making it impossible to get a gauge of pricing before going to contract.

The best way to feel confident in your purchase is by first determining your structural options with your sales rep. Once these are chosen, you'll know how much is left until you reach your max budget. Ask yourself the following questions:

- Are you comfortable with that amount left?
- Are you $5,000 away from your limit?
- Can you qualify for more? If so, how would that change your monthly cost?

You can ask the sales rep what the average buyer in the community spends on upgrades, but it's probably an unreliable number. I've watched people spend $5,000 to $120,000 in the same community.

If you're looking to spend minimally, then a standard house is probably your best option. Make sure you're familiar with what a standard house looks like. People that are close to reaching their max budget often go standard and move in with some equity. As long as they have a clear idea of what the standard house looks like, they're happy! They have great bones to work with and a house with warranties. People that don't have a clear idea of what a standard house looks like and just figure it'll be fine, are typically not happy.

It is important to go in with a budget and know you may not get everything. I'll let you in on a little secret. Here's where your relationship with the sales rep comes in handy. Sometimes there are homes in production with standards already in them. The sales reps should be familiar with these, as they walk through them regularly. If they're not too busy, they might take the time to show you the lots under construction. Additionally, the houses are typically not locked until close to closing. Do what you want with that information. :)

Fair warning - it's your responsibility to learn about standards and upgrades. If you complain to the builder that you didn't know or your sales rep didn't tell you, it won't get you anywhere. It may even state in your purchase agreement that nothing the sales rep says is legally binding.

As a sales rep, I occasionally was under the impression that something was standard and it wasn't. I would never intentionally mislead a buyer, but sometimes there are errors in the system. If this did happen, I would try my best to get it resolved fairly, but often my hands were tied. On the flip side, I've had times where I went over everything correctly and the buyer would claim I didn't mention something.

My advice is to always keep a paper trail. Even if you've already asked a question but don't have a reference of it in writing, follow up with the sales rep via email. I started doing this as a sales rep to protect not only the buyer, but my reputation as well. I hated for anything to fall through the cracks, or for the buyer to claim something false about me.

Unexpected Upgrades

There are many items that you would think are standard, but count as an upgrade. Here are some unexpected upgrades to keep an eye out for:

- Sink height
- Toilet height
- Powder room vanity
- Medicine cabinets
- Cabinet knobs
- Cabinet size
- Door sizes
- Door styles
- Second-floor height
- Refrigerator
- Washer and Dryer
- Kitchen backsplash
- Hose spigot in the backyard

CONTRACT

Once you have chosen a floor plan, lot, and discussed upgrades, you're almost there!

It's rare for the builder to hold a lot for you, but if you're feeling apprehensive, go through your list one more time. Don't rush a decision based on emotion. You want to feel confident about purchasing your new construction home!

NEGOTIATION & INCENTIVES

While it's common to negotiate a contract in real estate, builders rarely negotiate. The offer system that Realtors® use for resale is almost nonexistent in new homes. However, builders will sometimes offer extra incentives. As the prices of communities go up, builders may hit a lull in sales. To keep the momentum of the community going, buyers may add an incentive in the form of design center credit. It's usually minimal in the grand scheme of things and not worth waiting around for. It's maybe between $5,000 to $10,000 or $35 to $60 in a monthly payment.

The sales rep might have this incentive in their back pocket, but not necessarily tell you about it. Others might be more transparent and let you know. If a builder has an active waiting list or is hitting their monthly goal, don't count on an incentive.

So if you do plan to negotiate with the builder, just know it's almost always in the form of an incentive, and not off the total price of the home. The reason being that a large monetary negotiation could affect future appraisals in the community and look bad to investors. Your best chance at negotiation is if a home is close to being completed that was canceled. Builders do not want to sit on completed homes.

Once a community sells out, builders will sell their model homes. Models are loaded with upgrades and priced at the current base price. I have witnessed buyers negotiate the price, but at the end of the day, they're closing as one of the more expensive homes in the neighborhood, without a full warranty.

When it comes to negotiation, you never know until you ask. If you feel comfortable asking for an incentive, go for it, but don't expect it'll happen. Talk to your Realtor® and see where you stand based on the current housing market.

GOING TO CONTRACT

A contract is a legally binding document. The builder will use it to reference everything. Unfortunately, people don't always read it and try to negotiate afterward. Builders will not budge on this. They will not add or remove something just because you don't like it.

As I've mentioned before, the contract is written in a way to protect the builder. They can get away with this because new homes are in demand. So before you sign anything, make sure you understand what the terms are. If you need help with this, have someone you trust look it over.

The contract will also lay out some important details of the building process. If you find something in the contract that contradicts what the sales rep told you, double-check this before you sign. The contract will always stand.

The contract is sent out electronically. You will also get bombarded with disclosures at the same time. Your Realtor® should be able to walk you through this part of the process as well, but it helps to do your due diligence.

CHRISTINA ZAMORA | @thechristinazamora

CONGRATULATIONS ON YOUR NEW HOME!

Congratulations! Go take that insta worthy picture. You're on the way to a new home!

Once you've gone to contract, the process will be slightly different than purchasing a resale home. Instead of getting the keys to your new house, you'll be walking out of the office with a stack of papers. Enjoy the process, it's exciting to watch the progress as your home gets built.

As you wait for your home to close there will be a million questions and stressors that cross your mind. Remember to reflect on the reasons why you decided to build this home and not lose sight of that. Be sure to capture this moment and celebrate it with loved ones!

If you have a question, need an agent in CA or just want to say hi, let's chat. 720-227-1413

CHRISTINA ZAMORA | @thechristinazamora

CONTACT

 @THECHRISTINAZAMORA

CHRISTINA@REMAXENVISION.COM

720-227-1413

RE/MAX
ENVISION   DRE#02026883

ABOUT

Christina Zamora was born in Littleton, Colorado, and is the fourth child out of five. At a young age, Christina developed a love for entertaining others. She began competitive cheerleading and pursued it through high school. Shortly after graduating from Metropolitan State University with a BA in Business Management, Christina started working with a local home builder in new construction. While diving into real estate, Christina discovered her second love, volunteering. She served on the Young Professionals Chapter Board of Children's Hospital Colorado.

After three years of navigating Colorado real estate, her sense of adventure called her to California, where she quickly became a top producer at her company. Although new construction had proven fruitful, Christina saw a huge lack of buyer representation in the market and jumped on the opportunity.

Christina currently lives in Hollywood and strives to be her buyer and seller's top resource as a Realtor®. She continues to pursue her other two passions, acting + volunteering. In fact, a portion of proceeds from this eBook is going to A Light in Dark Places, which is a non-profit that uses performing arts to bring understanding, resources, and hope to those affected by suicide. In addition, Christina pledges to sponsor a meal in her client's name at the local Ronald McDonald House with every house closed. As her career grows, Christina plans to continue incorporating her business with her volunteer and giveback efforts.

Some of Christina's other interests include hiking, her dog Sir Maximo, Santiago's breakfast burritos, working out, window shopping, picnics on the beach, and trying all the sauces at restaurants.

CHRISTINA ZAMORA

ACKNOWLEDGEMENTS

As everyone can attest, 2020 was a difficult year. At Christmas, I cried over Facetime with a friend, as I reflected on how grateful I was to have my mom. She got COVID-19 in early December and I truly didn't know if I would see her again. Our relationship had been far from perfect, but we recently found peace, with a new horizon of memories to come. On New Year's Eve, I reflected upon this past year and my life, and I decided 2021 would be dedicated to my mom, as a celebration of her being alive. I fell asleep and woke up on Jan 1, 2021, with the idea to write this eBook, and at that moment I knew the birthday (February 9th) of my late brother, Rusty, would be the publishing target that would keep me accountable.

So, first things first. Thank you, Mom, for gracing me with the freedom to think on my own and for your continuous love. Thank you for having the audacity to have five kids and for giving me the most loving siblings. Thank you, Rusty, who continues to keep me accountable even from above. To Brittaney, Tiffaney, and Christian who never quit on me. To Vince, Chris, Bella, Abby, Vin, Champ, and Colt, who are my highlights of coming home.

To those who have seen out the variety of days: Hannah, Jessica, Kristin, Jamila, Courtney, and Clarissa. I couldn't live.

Two angels: Olivia Phan, my fellow CSHS alumni, for so kindly formatting, and Shahla Khan, with the incredible editing.

Last, but not least, thank you to the many women who have taken leaps of faith in me, and have provided me with the opportunities and stepping stones that helped get me where I am today. Most importantly, thank YOU for reading this.

I hope that we can chat soon.

Made in the USA
Las Vegas, NV
26 December 2022

64210619R00031